# COLORADO TODAY

## Influences from Many Cultures

Angelo Bitsis

NEW YORK

Published in 2016 by The Rosen Publishing Group, Inc.
29 East 21st Street, New York, NY 10010

Book Design: Iron Cupcake Design

Cataloging-in-Publication Data

Names: Bitsis, Angelo.
Title: Colorado today / Angelo Bitsis.
Description: New York : PowerKids Press, 2016. | Series: Spotlight on Colorado | Includes index.
Identifiers: ISBN 9781499415193 (pbk.) | ISBN 9781499415209 (6 pack) | ISBN 9781499415223 (library bound)
Subjects: LCSH: Colorado--Juvenile literature.
Classification: LCC F776.3 B58 2016 | DDC 978.8--dc23

Photo Credits: photo.ua/Shutterstock.com, cover; Images by Dr. Alan Lipkin/Shutterstock.com, 3; ljh images/Shutterstock.com, 4; Tom Tietz/iStock/Thinkstock, 5; AL PARKER PHOTOGRAPHY/ Shutterstock.com, 6; Atlaspix/Shutterstock.com, 7; reptiles4all/Shutterstock.com, 7; LC-USZ62-110874/loc.gov, 8; Joseph Becker/Library of Congress (digital id: cubcic brk7627)/ File:Chinese railroad workers sierra nevada.jpg/Wikimedia Commons, 10; bikeriderlondon/ Shutterstock.com, 11; LC-DIG-ggbain-15859/loc.gov, 13; Junial Enterprises/Shutterstock.com, 14; Doug Pensinger/Getty Images, 15; LC-DIG-fsa-8b27019/loc.gov, 16; © Everett Collection Historical/Alamy Stock Photo, 17; U.S. National Archives and Records Administration/Parker, Tom, Photographer (NARA record: 4682167/File:Granada Relocation Center, Amache, Colorado. A general all over view of a section of the emergency . . . - NARA - 539071.jpg/Wikimedia Commons, 18; LOT 3119/loc.gov, 20; Everett Historical/Shutterstock.com, 21; Everett Historical/ Shutterstock.com, 23; SNEHIT/Shutterstock.com, 24; Katherine Welles/Shutterstock.com, 25; Samot/ Shutterstock.com, 26; Arina P Habich/Shutterstock.com, 27; Arina P Habich/Shutterstock.com, 28; Alexander Gordeyev/Shutterstock.com, 28; iyd39/Shutterstock.com, 29; Harry How/Getty Images, 30; Brian Bahr/Getty Images/NHLI, 31; AP Photo/Ed Kosmicki, File, 33; AP Photo/The Pueblo Chieftain, Chris McLean, 34; Arina P Habich/Shutterstock.com, 35; Perspectives - Jeff Smith/ Shutterstock.com, 36; AP Photo/Brennan Linsley, 37; kojihirano/Shutterstock.com, 39; Phil Berry/ Shutterstock.com, 41; Alexey Kamenskiy/Shutterstock.com, 43; AnatBoonsawat/Shutterstock.com, 45.

Manufactured in the United States of America

CPSIA Compliance Information: Batch #BW16PK: For further information contact Rosen Publishing, New York, New York at 1-800-237-9932

# Contents

State Symbols                          4

People Make the State Great            8

A State of Immigrants                 12

Challenges of Diversity               16

Contributions                         20

Education                             24

The Colorado Lifestyle                26

Sports                                30

Festivals and Celebrations            34

First, Best, and Only                 38

Colorado by the Numbers               42

Fun Facts                             44

Glossary                              46

Index                                 48

# CHAPTER 1

# State Symbols

Colorado officially joined the Union on August 1, 1876, becoming a state 100 years after the signing of the Declaration of Independence. It is known as the **Centennial** State because of this. Since becoming a state, Colorado has adopted symbols to represent its **native** nature and culture.

*Rocky Mountain columbine*

In 1899, Colorado's **legislature** chose the Rocky Mountain columbine as the state flower. These white and **lavender** flowers grow around the state's mountains and are protected by law. While traveling by wagon in 1896, scholar A. J. Fynn saw these beautiful flowers growing in a meadow and was inspired

LARK BUNTING

In 1925, Colorado made it illegal for a person to gather more than 25 Rocky Mountain columbines in one day. The government wanted to make sure these delicate and rare flowers were around for future Coloradans to enjoy!

to write the song "Where the Columbines Grow." In 1915, "Where the Columbines Grow" became the official state song.

In 1931, the lark bunting became Colorado's official state bird. The lark bunting migrates to Colorado in April and stays until September, when it flies south for the winter. When in Colorado, these birds live on the plains and can even be found up to 8,000 feet (2,438 m) high in the mountains!

## ROCKY MOUNTAIN HIGH

After visiting the Rocky Mountains in Colorado, John Denver was inspired to write the song "Rocky Mountain High." John Denver was not his real name. He was born Henry John Deutschendorf Jr., but took the stage name John Denver after the capital city of Colorado. He loved Colorado and lived there for many years. In 2007, Colorado adopted "Rocky Mountain High" as its second official state song.

ROCKY MOUNTAIN BIGHORN SHEEP

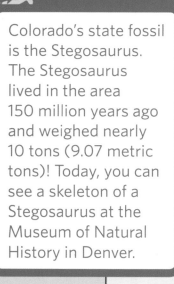

Colorado's state fossil is the Stegosaurus. The Stegosaurus lived in the area 150 million years ago and weighed nearly 10 tons (9.07 metric tons)! Today, you can see a skeleton of a Stegosaurus at the Museum of Natural History in Denver.

In 1961, Colorado adopted the Rocky Mountain bighorn sheep as its state animal. Bighorn sheep can weigh up to 300 pounds (136 kg) and have long, curving horns that they use for fighting each other. These animals are only found in the Rockies, a mountain range of more than 3,000 miles (4,800 km) that spans Colorado.

The state insect is the Colorado hairstreak butterfly, which has purple, black, and orange wings. It was named state insect in 1996 after fourth-grade students in Colorado asked their government to officially adopt it. In 2008, thanks to the efforts of fourth-grade students at Denver's Skyline Vista Elementary School, the western painted turtle became the state reptile. This turtle is found at ponds and lakes throughout Colorado.

The state motto is *Nil Sine Numine*. It is Latin for "Nothing Without the Deity" and is on the state seal. In 1911, Colorado created its state flag. It has two blue stripes representing the sky and a white stripe in the middle representing the snow that covers the peaks of the Rocky Mountains. The flag also includes a big red C that has a gold circle in the center, which stands for the sun and also for gold, in honor of the state's mining history.

WRANGLE UP SOME FACTS

Colorado's state tree is the Colorado blue spruce, which has a silver-blue color.

The western tiger salamander is Colorado's state amphibian. These salamanders have yellow and black stripes similar to a tiger's orange and black stripes.

The state of Utah got its name from the Ute people. Utah is Colorado's neighbor and is the location of the Uintah and Ouray Reservation, home of the Northern Ute Indian Tribe.

# CHAPTER 2

# People Make the State Great

Many different kinds of people have made Colorado the place it is today. The first people to live in the Colorado area were ancestors of Native Americans. Thousands of years ago, the Ancestral Puebloans lived in the southwest part of Colorado. More than a thousand years ago, the Ute people settled in Colorado. Two Ute tribes continue to live in the state and contribute to Colorado's culture. After the Ute,

*Ute men and women in Colorado, circa 1893*

other Native American groups moved into the area. These included the Kiowa, the Cheyenne, the Apache, and the Arapaho. They lived on the plains in the eastern part of the state, while the Ute mostly lived near the mountains and plateaus to the west. Hunting bison was important to the cultures of the Plains peoples.

Around 1541, a Spanish **expedition** led by explorer Francisco Vázquez de Coronado passed near present-day Colorado. In 1682, French explorer René-Robert Cavelier, Sieur de La Salle claimed the land for France after sailing down the Mississippi River. In 1706, a Spanish soldier named Juan de Ulibarrí actually set foot in Colorado and claimed it for Spain. At about this time, British colonists from New England and Virginia also began to claim the region. In 1803, France sold part of Colorado to the United States in the Louisiana Purchase. In 1848, the rest of Colorado was sold by Mexico to the United States through the Treaty of Guadalupe-Hidalgo. The influences of French, Spanish, and Mexican cultures can still be found in Colorado. The state's oldest town, San Luis, was founded in 1851 by Hispanic settlers.

## COLORADO'S ORIGINAL RESIDENTS

The Ute are the oldest continuously living culture in Colorado. Today, more than half of the Ute people live on reservations where they have their own tribal government. Colorado has two reservations: the Southern Ute Indian Reservation and the Ute Mountain Ute Tribe Reservation. Both are located in the southwestern part of the state.

## LANGUAGE LESSON!

"Maiku" (MY-kuh) means "hello" in the Ute language.

American pioneers started creating **settlements** in the 19th century. With the discovery of gold in 1858, **prospectors** began to show up, hoping to strike it rich. A few years later, railroads were built. Chinese and Japanese immigrants began arriving in Colorado. They helped the territory to grow by working on farms and building the railroads. With this new form of transportation, people were able to come to Colorado faster than ever before. As more people settled there, cities grew, eventually forming what we now know as Colorado.

*Chinese laborers worked throughout the American West. This drawing shows them working on a railroad during winter.*

At Colorado's current growth rate, its population is expected to reach 6 million by 2020.

*Colorado's population, like the population of the United States, is becoming more diverse.*

Today, more than 5 million people live in Colorado. Most of the population is Caucasian, or white. Almost 21 percent of the population is Hispanic. Mexicans make up the largest group within this Hispanic population. Black or African American people make up 4 percent of the population. About 3 percent of the population is people of Asian descent, while 1.6 percent of Colorado's people are Native American.

## KNOWLEDGE NUGGET

Spanish explorers called their newly discovered land "Colorado" because of the red-colored sandstone they found while exploring along the Colorado River. Colorado means "colored red" in Spanish. In 1861, the area became a U.S. territory, and the government decided to keep the name.

# CHAPTER 3

# A State of Immigrants

Colorado has always been a place where different cultures come together. Long before Europeans arrived, the Ute and other Native American cultures traded, fought, and mixed in the Rocky Mountains region and in the plains to the east. Before Colorado became a state, Spanish explorers, French traders, and American settlers left their mark, too.

Immigrants from European countries moved into Colorado alongside American-born settlers. Many of these first immigrants were Scandinavian, Irish, and Scottish. They had heard about new opportunities in the West and wanted a chance at a better life. Immigrants worked in mines and on railroads and farms. In the early 1900s, some railroad and mine workers began to **strike** because they felt their working conditions were unfair and unsafe. Immigrants from China, Italy, Germany, and Russia took some of the jobs on the railroads

## A SUCCESS STORY

Adolph Coors, owner of the famous Coors Brewing Company, emigrated from Germany to Golden, Colorado. Not knowing English and having no money, he stowed away on a ship traveling to Baltimore, Maryland. He decided to go West to make his fortune. And he did! Today, the Coors brewery in Golden is the largest single-site brewery in the world.

and mines. Often, railroad and mining companies would hire these new immigrants to replace striking workers. The new immigrants were less likely to strike because they needed money for their families. They also did not have the same rights as American citizens and did not want to upset the people giving them jobs. This caused conflict between immigrant groups. Some immigrants who had been there longer believed the new immigrants were taking their jobs. There were other conflicts, too. In 1914, in the Ludlow Massacre, mine owners attacked a camp of the striking immigrant workers, killing 5 miners, 2 women, and 12 children. This outraged the workers, who began fighting with company owners. The fighting got so bad that President Woodrow Wilson sent soldiers to stop the conflict.

*The aftermath of the Ludlow Massacre*

## FIGHTING FOR RIGHTS

Chin Lin Sou was an immigrant from China. He was one of the first Chinese people to move to Colorado. Like many Chinese immigrants, he worked on the railroad. Because he was fluent in both English and Chinese, he was given better jobs than most immigrants. Later, he worked as a mine supervisor and eventually bought his own store. He became a leader in the Chinese community and helped Chinese people gain rights in Colorado.

Today, Colorado's largest minority group is Hispanic. Mexicans, the largest immigrant population in the state, make up about 75 percent of the Hispanic population. People from African countries like Ethiopia are also moving to Colorado. This newer population often works in places that do not require specialized skills or full knowledge of the English language, like the meat-packing facilities of Colorado's cattle country. Others work at Colorado's ski resorts, and a growing number of educated Africans are seeking jobs in politics and places like universities. Like the immigrants of the past, they come for a better life and a chance to be a part of the Colorado community.

## DESTINATION: COLORADO

One out of ten residents of Colorado was born in a foreign country! One out of every nine workers in the state is an immigrant.

*Immigrants are an essential part of Colorado's culture and economy.*

Demonstrators wave U.S. and Mexican flags during a rally at the Colorado State Capitol to protest U.S. immigration laws.

# CHAPTER 4

# Challenges of Diversity

By 1868, the Ute and other tribes had a large reservation in western Colorado. After miners found gold and silver on parts of the reservation, the U.S. government took away much of the land in 1874.

After the Louisiana Purchase, fights began between Native Americans and white settlers. Many Native Americans felt settlers were invading their land. Settlers believed they had a right to be there. In 1881, the U.S. government began forcing the Ute people onto **reservations**. Reservation life was terrible. Many people died from disease or starvation.

RESERVATION

Native American children were taken from their families and forced to go to boarding schools taught by white people. Without children to pass their traditions on to, Native American cultures were in danger of dying out. Today, many Ute people live on reservations, but they have more say in what happens to them. They have their own tribal governments that lead their people in the ways they want.

*The National Association for the Advancement of Colored People (NAACP) met in Denver in 1925 to combat racism in Colorado.*

African Americans also faced **discrimination** in Colorado. Throughout the West, African Americans were not allowed to do many things that white people could. They were not allowed to stay in hotels, ride on stagecoaches, or vote. In the 20th century, new laws ended discrimination, but challenges remained. African American and Hispanic children usually ended up in different schools than Caucasian children, a form of **segregation**. In 1973, the **Supreme Court** heard the case of *Keyes v. School District No. 1, Denver*. This led Colorado to desegregate its public schools.

Justina Ford became Denver's first female African American doctor in 1902. She attended medical school, but was denied a medical license because she was a woman and an African American. Determined to treat patients, Ford began practicing medicine at her home. She treated patients of all races, even when they couldn't afford to pay her. She learned several languages to talk to patients who didn't speak English. Her home is now the Black American West Museum.

*The Granada Relocation Center during World War II*

Asians in Colorado experienced difficulties from the time they arrived in the 19th century. In 1882, the United States passed a law banning Chinese immigrants from citizenship. In 1942, during World War II, the federal government opened a Japanese internment camp called the Granada Relocation Center, or "Amache," near Granada, Colorado. Japanese people were imprisoned here because the

United States was at war with Japan. More than 7,000 Japanese people, most of them American citizens, lived here until 1945 when the camp was closed.

Before it was sold to the United States with the Treaty of Guadalupe-Hidalgo, part of Colorado was owned by Mexico. The U.S. government agreed to let Mexicans living in Colorado become American citizens. After the purchase, they went back on their promise. Many Mexicans stayed and tried to make their fortunes anyway. They often faced discrimination. In the 1960s, the Chicano Movement began in Pueblo, Colorado. "Chicano" is a term some Mexican American people call themselves. At the time, many business owners refused to hire Mexican Americans, leaving families in poverty. The Chicano Movement **boycotted** racist companies and protested racist policies. While discrimination still exists, the Chicano Movement has gained rights and respect for Mexican Americans in Colorado and across the United States.

Rodolfo "Corky" Gonzalez was a leader of the Chicano Movement in Colorado. He got his first taste of politics when he registered voters under John F. Kennedy's presidential campaign. He registered more Mexican Americans to vote than any other person in Colorado's history. He also started the civil rights organization Crusade for Justice.

Federico Peña became the first Hispanic mayor of Denver in 1983. He beat out the favored William H. McNichols Jr., who had served for 14 years. Mayor Peña was so loved that he won a second term, too!

# CHAPTER 5

# Contributions

HELEN HUNT JACKSON

As difficult as life was in the "Wild West," many Coloradans fought to create better conditions for others in Colorado and throughout the United States. In 1881, Colorado **activist** Helen Hunt Jackson wrote *A Century of Dishonor*. This book showed the terrible conditions Native American people were forced to live in. It started people across the country talking about the poor treatment of Native Americans.

### KNOWLEDGE NUGGET

Helen Hunt Jackson paid to have *A Century of Dishonor* published. The book described how the U.S. government mistreated Native Americans, including broken treaties. She sent copies to every member of Congress.

Activist Caroline Churchill spoke out for women's rights. She started *The Colorado Antelope* newspaper, later called the *Queen Bee*. She used it to discuss discrimination against women. Some people found this shocking because, at the time, women did not get involved in politics. Churchill paved the way for women to win the right to vote in Colorado in 1893. Women had worked hard for many years to gain the vote in Colorado. Their efforts pushed the country to extend voting rights to women in 1920.

To gain the right to vote, women in Colorado printed leaflets, gave speeches, wrote letters, and went door-to-door to argue their views. After they won, women voters and activists fought for better schools and improved working conditions, helping to change Colorado from a series of rough mining towns into a functioning society.

*Colorado governor Oliver H. Shoup signs a document to ratify the 19th Amendment granting women the right to vote in December 1919.*

Barney L. Ford left behind a life of slavery thanks to the Underground Railroad, a secret network of people that helped slaves to escape slavery and into places where they could live safely.

Barney L. Ford helped to improve Colorado for African Americans. He escaped slavery in Virginia and headed to Colorado in 1860. He wanted to buy a mine, but was not allowed to own one because of his race. Determined to succeed, he opened several businesses instead. After becoming successful, he fought for civil and voting rights for African Americans. He even helped block Colorado from gaining statehood because U.S. laws at the time said that African Americans were not allowed to vote. In 1865, after going to Washington, D.C., he convinced the government to agree to let African American people vote in Colorado.

Coloradans like Molly and J. J. Brown worked to improve life for workers and the poor. The Browns were rich mine owners, but they weren't always rich. Molly's parents were poor Irish immigrants. The Browns bought mines rich in silver and became wealthy. Never forgetting how difficult being poor was, Molly used her influence to help others. When the *Titanic* sank, she convinced the rich survivors to donate money to the poor ones who had lost everything they had in the sinking.

After the Ludlow Massacre, where a mine company killed workers and their families, Molly became an **advocate** for workers' rights. She convinced John D. Rockefeller Jr., a rich mine owner, to grant workers more freedoms. The Ludlow Massacre helped the American people see how difficult life was for poor workers. Congress created new laws to allow workers to join **labor unions** and to limit the workday to eight hours.

MOLLY BROWN

African Americans made up a large portion of the pioneers who moved to Colorado. One out of every three Coloradan cowboys was African American!

## KNOWLEDGE NUGGET

Unsinkable Molly Brown was on the *Titanic* and survived after it crashed into an iceberg and sank. Not wanting to leave anyone behind, she forced her lifeboat to turn around and search for survivors in the water. A Denver gossip columnist reporting the story gave her the nickname the "Unsinkable Mrs. Brown."

# CHAPTER 6

# Education

In 1859, Colorado's first "school" was opened by Owen J. Goldrick. Called Union School, it was a small classroom in Denver. In 1860, the first schoolhouse was built in Boulder. In 1862, the first tax-supported, or public, schools opened in Denver.

Schools in the countryside were one-room or two-room log cabins where one teacher instructed students of different ages. City schools were often

The Morrill Land Act was signed into law by President Abraham Lincoln on July 2, 1862. This is the first instance of the federal government giving aid for higher education. Western territories were now able to build colleges. Before this, higher education was something only wealthy families could afford. With the passing of this law, farmers and other working people had the opportunity to go to college.

*This historic Colorado schoolhouse stands in the shadow of the Rocky Mountains.*

In 1898, the first female student graduated from the Colorado School of Mines. In 2015, 27 percent of the enrolled students were female.

larger, with several rooms and teachers. In the 1930s, U.S. government programs gave money to states for education. Modern schools, like the ones most children attend today, were built. Today, more than 850,000 students learn in Colorado public schools!

Colorado's oldest college, the University of Denver, opened in 1864 as Colorado Seminary. In 1862, the Morrill Land Act gave federally owned land to states to build colleges, as long as they taught agriculture, engineering, or military training. Colorado Agricultural College, today called Colorado State University, opened its doors in 1870. With little money, it wasn't until 1879 that it accepted only five students! In 1874, the Colorado School of Mines began teaching

engineering with a focus on mining. In 1876, the University of Colorado was founded. It had only two teachers and 44 students! Today, thousands of students from across the country and the world attend Colorado's universities.

Nicknamed the "Professor," Owen J. Goldrick was an eccentric but beloved man. He was known for his showy clothes and way of talking. Townspeople said he would curse at his horses in Latin!

# CHAPTER 7

# The Colorado Lifestyle

**SNOWBOARDER**

Coloradans enjoy staying active through outdoor activities. They love the outdoors, and it's no wonder. They live in one of the most beautiful places on Earth! Coloradans can be found hunting, fishing, hiking, bicycling, golfing, camping, and horseback riding. Skiing and snowboarding are popular sports in winter. Colorado is world famous for its skiing and snowboarding. The state has nearly 30 ski resorts, including some of the largest in the nation. The two most visited ski resorts in the United States, Vail Mountain and Breckenridge Ski Resort, are both in Colorado.

Snowboarding became popular in the 1960s after an American invented an early version of the snowboard called a "Snurfer" (short for "snow surfer").

*Farmers' markets, like this one in Parker, Colorado, provide fresh, local fruits and vegetables.*

Colorado has one of the lowest **obesity** rates in the United States. In 2013, only 21 percent of Coloradans were obese, while 28 percent of Americans were obese. Compared to the average American, the average Coloradan eats more fruits and vegetables, exercises more, drinks less soda, and spends less time sitting in front of the television.

## A CENTURY OF SKIING

How did skiing become so big in Colorado? In 1911, ski expert Carl Howelsen of Norway impressed the people of Hot Sulphur Springs, Colorado, by skiing down the side of a mountain and building a ski ramp to launch himself into the air. Almost overnight, skiing became a big draw in Colorado!

Boulder has more than 300 miles (483 km) of bike paths.

RENTAL BIKES AT UNION STATION

Many cities encourage an active lifestyle and promote eco-friendly activities. In the city of Boulder, bicycling is a favorite activity. Many people walk or bike to school or work. Bicycling is so popular that, when it snows heavily, it is not unusual for the city to plow the Boulder Creek bicycle path before plowing the roads!

*The Rocky Mountains provide a beautiful backdrop for a day of biking!*

Four out of five Coloradans live in cities, but they are surrounded by the natural beauty of mountains and parks. This allows Coloradans to have the best of both worlds. The state capital of Denver has the largest city park system in the United States. It has more than 200 parks within the city and 14,000 acres (5,665 ha) of mountain parks nearby.

*Colorado has 42 state parks and 13 national forests and grasslands that are perfect for hiking.*

Culture and the arts are popular with Coloradans, too. When they are not outdoors, Coloradans love to go to symphonies, ballets, operas, art galleries, and museums. There are many festivals and parades, too. It would be difficult to get bored in such a beautiful and interesting place!

**KNOWLEDGE NUGGET**

While only 37 percent of Americans live close to a park, 60 percent of Coloradans do!

# CHAPTER 8

# Sports

DENVER NUGGETS

Coloradans' active lifestyle can be seen in their love of sports. Colorado is unique because its capital city, Denver, has a professional team for every major sport. The Denver Broncos play football in the National Football League (NFL), the Colorado Avalanche play hockey in the National Hockey League (NHL), the Colorado Rockies play baseball for Major League Baseball (MLB), the Denver Nuggets play basketball for the National Basketball Association (NBA), and the Colorado Rapids play soccer for Major League Soccer (MLS).

## A HIGH SCORE IN THE MILE HIGH CITY

On December 13, 1983, the Denver Nuggets played the Detroit Pistons. The Nuggets lost 186–184, but the game went into triple overtime. It remains the highest-scoring game in NBA history!

Denver also has two pro lacrosse teams: the Denver Outlaws, who play outdoor lacrosse for Major League Lacrosse (MLL), and the Colorado Mammoths, who play indoor lacrosse for the National Lacrosse League (NLL). Colorado teams have won several national championships. The Denver Broncos won the Super Bowl in 1997 and 1998. The Colorado Avalanche won the Stanley Cup in 1996 and 2001.

## HALL OF FAMERS

Four Denver Broncos players are in the Pro Football Hall of Fame: John Elway, Floyd Little, Gary Zimmerman, and Shannon Sharpe.

*Colorado Avalanche players celebrate their Stanley Cup victory in 2001.*

The Pikes Peak International Raceway in Fountain, Colorado, has been a major auto-racing track since 1997.

Becky Hammon played college basketball for Colorado State University. She went on to become one of the most successful players in the Women's National Basketball Association (WNBA). When she retired, Hammon was offered a job as a full-time assistant coach for the NBA's San Antonio Spurs in 2014. This was the first time a woman had ever coached full-time for a major pro basketball, football, baseball, or hockey team!

Colorado is a perfect place for winter sports. In 1970, Denver won the bid to host the 1976 Winter Olympics. However, they did not end up hosting the games. The people of Colorado felt it would be too expensive and the extra people would add too much pollution. But it was an honor to be selected! Skiing is a popular activity for both ordinary Coloradans and professional athletes. Colorado has hosted the Alpine World Ski Championships four times, most recently in 2015. People from all over the world come to compete in ski jumping, cross-country skiing, and snowboarding.

Colorado's natural wonders make it one of the best states for hiking and biking. With the Rocky Mountains running through the middle of the state, Colorado is also perfect for mountain, rock, and ice climbing. The state has mountains for both beginners and experts, including Mount Elbert, the highest peak in the Rocky Mountains.

The official state sport of Colorado may surprise you. During Colorado's gold rush, the pack burro, or donkey, was used to haul

The 2015 Alpine World Ski Championships in Vail and Beaver Creek, Colorado, were watched by more than 800 million people worldwide.

supplies to and from mines. Because burros would be loaded with supplies, people could not ride them. Instead, the animals had to be walked. Legend has it that two miners struck gold in the same mine. They both raced to town to claim the mine for themselves. Since their burros were loaded with supplies, they had to run and pull the animals along behind them. To honor their unique history, Colorado has made pack burro racing the official state sport! Several Colorado towns hold pack burro races throughout the year.

PACK BURRO RACING

Mike the Headless Chicken Day might be Colorado's strangest festival. On September 10, 1945, farmer Lloyd Olsen went out to kill a rooster for dinner. He swung his ax and chopped Mike's head off. Instead of becoming dinner that night, Mike went on to live 18 months without a head! Fruita, Colorado, holds a festival every year to celebrate this odd event.

# CHAPTER 9

# Festivals and Celebrations

No day passes without a special event or celebration happening somewhere in Colorado. Coloradans celebrate their Statehood Day, or anniversary of becoming a state, every August 1. Each year, people flock to the Colorado State Fair and Rodeo in Pueblo, Colorado, the state's biggest summer event. It includes live music, rides, livestock shows, and attractions that highlight Colorado's ranching history.

COLORADO STATE FAIR

*Ice climbers show off their skills during Colorado's annual Ouray Ice Festival.*

A hot air balloon festival in Colorado is an extraordinary sight to see, especially at night when the balloons glow like giant, colorful lanterns!

Every January, the Ouray Ice Festival in Ouray, Colorado, brings together the world's best ice climbers. This exciting sport involves climbing glaciers. Hot air balloon festivals, held in Snowmass and other cities, are also popular. Colorado's beautiful landscape, with its towering mountains and open meadows, is even more impressive when viewed from a hot air balloon!

*The streets of Denver fill up every year for the Taste of Colorado Festival.*

Colorado is famous for its arts, music, and film festivals. Every September, the Telluride Film Festival showcases some of the year's best films. The state is home to many food festivals, such as the Pueblo Chile and Frijoles Festival, which celebrates the spicy chile pepper native to Pueblo, Colorado. Denver's Taste of Colorado Festival is an outdoor food and music festival that often draws in more than half a million people.

Besides festivals, Coloradans also honor the memories of people who have gone through **hardships** or have done great things through sacrifice. Every year, Coloradans **commemorate** the Sand Creek Massacre at the Sand Creek Massacre National Historic Site. On November 29, 1864, a troop of 675 men led by Col. John Chivington slaughtered nearly

Cesar Chavez successfully negotiated one of the first farmworkers' contracts, giving farmworkers protections they didn't have before. Although it is not a federal holiday, President Barack Obama has declared May 31st National Cesar Chavez Day. On this day, Chavez is honored for his work toward improving the lives of others.

The Crested Butte Wildflower Festival includes nature hikes that highlight the beautiful flowers of Colorado's mountain regions.

*Coloradans gather on the steps of the state capitol on the anniversary of the Sand Creek Massacre.*

200 peaceful Cheyenne and Arapaho people. This event began the Plains Indian Wars and damaged peace talks between the Native American Plains peoples and the United States.

Each January, Denver hosts the Martin Luther King Jr. March and Parade, or "Marade." It is the largest MLK rally in the country, attracting tens of thousands of people every year. Colorado is one of three states to recognize Cesar Chavez Day as a state holiday. Cesar Chavez was an important figure in securing farm laborers' rights. His work inspired other people to fight for workers' rights.

**37**

# CHAPTER 10

# First, Best, and Only

Colorado has a history like no other. Many "firsts" have taken place in the state. Colorado was the first state to grant women the right to vote by popular election in 1893. It was also the first to elect women to its state legislature. The first Stegosaurus dinosaur fossils were found in Morrison, Colorado. The world's first rodeo was held in Deer Trail, Colorado, in 1869, with cowboys competing for prizes. Mesa Verde National Park near Cortez, Colorado, is the first national park created to preserve human works rather than natural features. The park features a city built into the side of a cliff by the Ancestral Puebloan people.

Colorado has other claims to fame. Colorado Springs has the lowest obesity rate of any community in America. Grand Mesa in Colorado is the largest flat-top mountain on Earth.

## COLORADO'S ANCIENT INHABITANTS

The Ancestral Puebloan people lived at Mesa Verde for more than 700 years. That is five times longer than Colorado has been a state.

MESA VERDE NATIONAL PARK

Colorado's mountainous region is six times the size of Switzerland!

Colorado was the first state to have a separate court system for children. In 1903, the Denver Juvenile Court began hearing cases. Before this, children and adults were seen as the same in the eyes of the law.

Glenwood Springs, Colorado, has the world's largest hot springs pool. It is more than two blocks long! Half a billion dollars worth of gold has been mined in Central City, which is why it is known as the "Richest Square Mile on Earth." Canyon of the Ancients National Monument in Colorado contains more than 6,000 archaeological sites, the most in the United States. The road to the peak of Mount Evans reaches 14,260 feet (4,346 m) above sea level, making it the highest paved road in North America. Pikes Peak Railway is the highest railway in North America. Royal Gorge Bridge near Cañon City is the world's highest suspension bridge. At 10,430 feet (3,180 m) in elevation, Leadville, Colorado, is the highest city in the country.

Colorado is also a unique place. It is the only state to ever turn down the Olympics. The Kit Carson County Carousel in Burlington, Colorado, is the only antique carousel to still have its original paint. You can still ride it today! Colorado's southwestern corner touches three other states, making it the only place in the United States where four states meet.

## SACRED SPRINGS

The hot springs at Glenwood Springs were once a sacred place for members of the Ute tribe. They would take an annual pilgrimage, or journey, to bathe in the springs. Today, they are the site of a spa.

WRANGLE UP SOME FACTS

Though Pikes Peak Railway is one of the highest in the world, it has a perfect safety record.

ROYAL GORGE

# CHAPTER 11

# Colorado by the Numbers

- Colorado is home to 58 "fourteeners." Fourteeners are mountain peaks that are more than 14,000 feet (4,267 m) tall.

- Colorado has more than 1,000 mountain peaks at least two miles (3.2 km) high.

- Denver is known as the Mile High City. The 13th step of the Colorado State Capitol building in Denver is 5,280 feet (1,609 m), or exactly one mile, above sea level, making the city's nickname very appropriate.

- Because of the state's high **altitude**, a golf ball flies 10 percent farther in Colorado than in other places!

- Colorado is home to more than 960 wildlife species.

- Colorado has about 1,000 ghost towns!

**KNOWLEDGE NUGGET**

Many of Colorado's spooky, empty ghost towns are open for tours. Most have a only few buildings left standing.

Denver is the 23rd most populated American city. More than half a million people live there.

MOUNTAINS OF COLORADO

- The Rocky Mountains in Colorado are home to more than 9,600 miles (15,449 km) of fishing streams and 2,850 lakes.

- Colorado has four national parks: Mesa Verde National Park, Rocky Mountain National Park, Great Sand Dunes National Park and Preserve, and Black Canyon of the Gunnison National Park.

- The Colorado Trail is a hiking trail that is 500 miles (805 km) long. It crosses five river systems, six wilderness areas, seven national forests, and eight mountain ranges!

Some of Colorado's cities are so high up that visitors can get altitude sickness. This includes headaches and shortness of breath caused by the thin air at high elevations. The sickness usually goes away after a day or two.

# CHAPTER 12

# Fun Facts

- Denver receives 300 days of sunshine per year. That's more than San Diego, California, or Miami, Florida!

- Due to a political squabble in March 1905, Colorado had three governors in one day: first Alva Adams, then James H. Peabody, and finally Jesse F. McDonald.

- Scott Carpenter, one of the first American astronauts, named his space capsule *Aurora 7* after the streets he grew up on: Aurora Avenue and 7th Avenue in Boulder, Colorado.

- The Denver Mint can make more than 50 million coins every day. The mint opened in 1863 as a place for miners to bring gold dust and nuggets to be melted into bars. In 1906, it became an official U.S. mint, one of only four in the nation.

## COLORADO COMPANIES

Celestial Seasonings, the most popular brand of natural teas in North America, was started in 1969 in Boulder. Chipotle Mexican Grill, one of the most popular American fast food restaurant chains, was started in 1993 in Denver.

Do you have a coin handy? Take a look at it. If it has a small letter "D" engraved on the front, it was made at the Denver Mint!

*If you hike to the top of Pikes Peak, you'll be rewarded with a gorgeous view!*

- The cheeseburger was reportedly invented at the Humpty Dumpty Barrel Drive-In restaurant in Denver in 1935.

- On a trip to the summit of Pikes Peak, author Katharine Lee Bates was inspired to write "America the Beautiful." She wrote it as a poem, but it later became one of America's most popular patriotic songs.

"When I saw the view, I felt great joy. All the wonder of America seemed displayed there."
—Katharine Lee Bates on reaching the top of Pikes Peak

# Glossary

**activist**—A person who fights for social change.

**advocate**—A person who speaks for others' rights.

**altitude**—A measure of how high something is above sea level.

**boycotted**—Refused to buy or use a product or company as a political protest.

**centennial**—A 100-year period of time.

**commemorate**—To honor the memory of people involved in a tragic event.

**discrimination**—Treating a person or group of people unfairly because they are different.

**expedition**—A journey to explore new land.

**hardships**—Extremely difficult experiences.

**labor unions**—Organizations that protect workers' rights.

**lavender**—Light purple.

**legislature**—The group of people that make laws for a state or country.

**native**—Original to a region or area.

**obesity**—The condition of being very overweight and unhealthy.

**prospectors**—People who look for mineral deposits such as gold.

**reservations**—Lands set aside by the U.S. government that Native American groups were forced to live on.

**segregation**—Not giving people of different races access to the same places.

**settlements**—Places where people build a community or town.

**strike**—The deliberate act of stopping work in order to create wanted change in the workplace.

**Supreme Court**—The highest court in the United States.

# Index

**A**
African American, 11, 17, 22–23
Ancestral Puebloans, 8, 38
Arapaho, 9, 36

**B**
Brown, Molly, 22–23

**C**
celebrations, 34
Chicano Movement, 19
Cheyenne, 9, 36
Chin Lin Sou, 13
Chinese, 10, 12–13, 18
Churchill, Caroline, 21
Coors, Adolph, 12

**F**
festivals, 29, 34–37
Ford, Barney L., 22
Ford, Justina, 17

**G**
gold, 7, 10, 16, 32–33, 40, 44
Goldrick, Owen J., 24–25
Gonzalez, Rodolfo "Corky," 19

**H**
Hispanic, 9, 11, 14, 17, 19

**I**
immigrants, 10, 12–15, 18, 22

**J**
Jackson, Helen Hunt, 20
Japanese, 10, 18–19

**L**
Ludlow Massacre, 13, 23

**M**
Mexican Americans, 19
Mexicans, 9, 11, 14–15, 19
miners, 13, 16, 33, 44
Morrill Land Act, 24–25

**N**
Native Americans, 8–9, 11–12, 16, 20, 37

**P**
parks, 29, 38, 43
Peña, Federico, 19
pioneers, 10, 23
prospectors, 10

**R**
railroads, 10, 12–13
reservations, 8–9, 16
Rocky Mountains, 5–7, 12, 24, 28, 32, 43

**S**
sports, 26, 30, 32
state symbols, 4–7

**U**
University of Denver, 25
Ute, 8–9, 12, 16, 40

Due to the changing nature of Internet links, the Rosen Publishing Group, Inc., has developed an online list of websites related to the subject of this book. This site is updated regularly. Please use this link to access the list:
http://www.powerkidslinks.com/soco/ct